STROKES OF LIGHT

By the same author

Liquescence (1996)
Feathered Tongues (2004)

STROKES OF LIGHT

LUCY ALEXANDER

RECENT
WORK
PRESS

Strokes of Light
Recent Work Press
Canberra, Australia

Copyright © Lucy Alexander, 2020

ISBN: 9780648834304(paperback)

 A catalogue record for this book is available from the National Library of Australia

All rights reserved. This book is copyright. Except for private study, research, criticism or reviews as permitted under the Copyright Act, no part of this book may be reproduced, stored in a retrieval system, or transmitted in any form by any means without prior written permission. Enquiries should be addressed to the publisher.

Cover design: Recent Work Press
Set by Recent Work Press

recentworkpress.com

SS

To my family, all of you.

Contents

Part 1: Strokes of Light

Paper Giant	3
Pinch	4
Strokes Of Light	5
Deathcap	6
Swift	7
Fortune	8
Scoop	9
Mystic	10
Sleep	11
Eye	12
Skull	13
Cold	14
Floodplain	15

Part 2: Childpoems

Summer	19
Winter	20
Blood	21
For The World To Swing	22
Wildflower Seed Mix	23
River Child	24
Sea Child	25
Sky Child	26
Rabbit on the Moon	27
Washing in Winter	28
Iron My Breath	29
Before You Sleep	30
Coax	31

Part 3: Flight From Gravity

Apostle Bird	34
Crow	35
Magpie	36
Rooster	37
Cat	38
Dog	39
Borer	40
Snake	41
Amanita Muscaria	42
In Black	43
Yam Dream	44
Spurge	45
Jet Plane Year	46

Part 4: Luminous Things

Four	49
Dusk (Sundowner's Syndrome)	50
Zero	51
Breaking	52
Divers	53
Pears	54

Afterword	57

PART 1
STROKES OF LIGHT

Paper Giant

I will make you a paper giant. His head will go looming clouds; his bamboo bones crosshatch shadows; the tapers of his finger tips will reap sky; his canoe-feet tread furrows in the darkling soil. At night he will glow: one hundred tea lights spilling fire from his belly. He will learn motion and will run above your head, out of the reach of your shadow let down out of the sky. He will go picking stars, a stream of luminous points until he has a lit cathedral. Earth's sunset will eat his silhouette completely. Automaton can only fly so high, but bleach this light into memory, go searching for those huge prints in the shallow mud, find the ash and ember, flickering there to remind you it was real.

Pinch

Never relative the ones you love, never love the ones you study, never open the door if you know who is there and be sure to love the door. Always pinch the bigger half, if you can carry it. Always love your relatives and study them for uncertain opportunities. Always look through the crack between the door and its jamb before you open it fully - it will be a relative, a witch, or nothing but the wind. It will always be hard to tell the difference. Always take a pinch of a dream if you find one. Pinch dreamers. Never choose an aqua coloured door that is blue. Never argue it is green. Never love the aqua wind. Always prefer the certain door. Never study a pinch, never dream the wind, always wind the relatives, always pinch the study. Always, always without fail, love the witch.

Strokes Of Light

Here the brushstrokes are all downwards, like rain that comes in as thick as hard pressed crayon. The old house certainly a witch's with owls nesting in the cloven roof beams, their eyes the glimpse of paper beneath the overworked surface. A slim trespasser lights a match on her shoe and counts seconds between the warning strokes of light tearing up sky, before touching it to the paper. Smoke flies out the chimney - all fear no heat, gone without even leaving dents in the shading where ink might find a place to pool. The girl knows she must not lick the sugared hearth while fire takes up the air. An old woman's memory is ash in the oven. The sweet she knows would hit the tongue like magic.

Deathcap

The witch still shuttles through dreamscapes, doesn't matter how many times she is told she is not there. Fire, the mocker of magic, flares among the graphite smoke; trespassing again and again on memory's chimney. But here she come again hurtling through the void where the thought of her would have been if she had not taken the space for herself, as black as a cave and more empty. Her eyes are worked until they shine. Her fingers telescope beyond their ends. Poisonous —just the way she was made.

Swift

In a cup made for flesh she stopped and left a beaky blemish. Seen how moths have feathers, too? They twirl full moon-dieting on their hope for another moth; the bird against breast-pocket may have flown a million miles in the dark; traced the atlas of her voice over the wind above the dark water searching the world's wingbeat-measured reaches for another wind-rider. Here, high windows showed sky that knew her name so she fought against their panes, the light and wind of her life unfolding a ceiling away. This mammal tender part warm-folding against its twin's skin was not enough softness to hold a swift egg-child; the chirping love-wing; a wind-bird who curled her claws and let the great unstopped stillness swoop down to press her heart closed.

Fortune

Stepping from the train in Cordoba they ran to me, several of them, elbowing one another. The older one with blotted eyes spoke strong and river fast. Her teeth collected consonants; I could not separate her words. Then, she held out the rosemary, leaves splayed to scenting her fingers that rested a moment, familiar, on my clavicle. The pang of green stems, was it magic? How had this dialled up long gone days and got between the layers of my own damn skin to lie there dormant and ready to be called. A crush of salvia in a distant city. When she told the future she only eroded my belief, hushing her daughters and shaking her shawl. The leaves abandoned their scent and stopped me. I am still there, although 'She understands,' they exhaled and I drew in. They pulled my straps, I nodded pushing onwards began my walk into the broken distance.

Scoop

The moon holds a scoop of darkness out to the sky. It's been waiting years to crest the horizon; an exact sideways punch; a pregnancy, concave to ladle up black blue. It promises a lit crescent doorway. An invitation to gaze down shadow-melt, learn the moon's secret word for itself...could a taste of that cure us all?

Mystic

It's not easy being a mystic these days. Too much data to drink gradually; no time to taste blasted stars or poke in the pockets of your mind until you cough up ancestral memories. Also, there's been too much benefiting from another's loss. You think a chain of changes will only lead to a peak where you have amassed all the pretty coins. But, you can only exchange them for nothing—and then, well then, it is your turn to lose and another's quick hand will reach for you in falling and catch the exhumed oxygen of your loss (smell it now?) and all you tinkling belongings. There's nothing to be gained by saying this over and again; no one hears, even if they know it to be true. This air smells metallic and full of exhaustion.

Sleep

The future is surely made of sleep. Soft stuff of drip down cloud effect, bottle body drowsy, chimed with silence, doused with absence. The future forms from the past—dropping into moment after moment. We will be content with empty as there's no choice but flit high but lay down low. She was not asleep, her face the rigid calm of not being there, after her family sang all night for three nights and the monks came and went taking their robes and the waft of incense. We send kites into the sky, we send paper cranes into the river, we send poems into the void between skin and synapse, we send ourselves into unknown sleep, so deep it pays no dividends.

Eye

I throw my eye up to the sky, notice that spill of air against blue temper in the wind. Today the horsetail flume means change, I smell it, too, hubris, arrow points of moisture in atmospheric pressure to the north. The gentlemen cirrus nod to flying birds as they turn to speckles on the deep horizon strung on the possibility of their wings, beads along lines of air, catching the updraft and whorling there. My eye sees aquamarine circles, spindrift weather, water's dance with heat from ice to liquid, liquid to steam. My eye fills like a pond that I drink back down to earth.

Skull

Just beyond your sideways glance there are always suspended constellations. They are whirling axis data motes, thoughts thrown, spun on pitch-slide of now, whole galaxies of petrified bones forming pinhole lights that sting their way through the skull you are sealed in. They hover - looking a distant purple-green from so close and seem promise something beyond the stifle of love, outside the cotton-wooled mind, each one a tunnel to a new possible, each one a kiss on your solid brow.

Cold

It takes a moment to realise it is the smell of cold. Cold like old brick dust that settled long ago. Or the snuff of snow on the wind. Cold of air that lay against water. Cold of stone lying under that stream. It is a sour sweet, like green tea on the tongue - the cooler it gets the more bitter it becomes. But that very bitterness welling up from tongue to thought, a wince of flavour with a bite of insistence that turns aside. Is it a catalogue of sufferings - many of them small, that prick and pummel at memory's gate? Here, watching the pale day, lips blue for kissing. There, the frozen river that cannot move. A nip in the nostril. With fingers mauve and dampened by ice. To recall now that perhaps it's not the smell but how it feels.

Floodplain

The floodplain is full of the black earth we are made of. All of the world's particles pass through this zone: yours, too. Have them arranged so your heart can weigh in. Have them in order, crystallised and formatted. The light frothing up will hold your new name. Hurry to smear this stinking mud all over your life events: erase them all. Know yourself as you are for the last time. Even as we watch you are changing, hadron by hadron, boson and fermion the electron and neutron flying to new positions. If light is congealing, know it is the end: of skin against earth; against the salute of the era. Have your memories boxed in terabytes. Have your fingerprints hankering for a new atomic arrangement. And then there is nothing to recall.

PART 2
CHILDPOEMS

Summer

My childhood was full of summer,
the sky riddled blue
and tiny cicadas clicked and hummed
as if they held out heat in their voices.
Beaches stretched white rimmed forever
to the cusp of indigo horizon
so distant it shocked your eyes
into seeing mirage islands
and reams of crinkled fish.
Grass dried into crisp arrangements
clattered in the breezes—if they came.
Heat was everywhere and ripened the orchard fruit
all powdery and fresh
our own spotted apricots and dripping plums.
If we were quiet we could taste our grandmother's loganberries
read books in the pear tree
till bedtime came and went
and we were deliciously called home.
In the evening the sea was smooth enough—even for my cousins—
green and cool as their promises to write:
It was always like this.

Winter

My childhood
was full of winter.
Afternoons of grass and kindling
for fire's warmth in evenings.
Shadow and the crack of laurel
in the heat.
My father cut great swathes
and each year on my birthday
we'd flatten an un-mown path
and pile it high to pop and spit
like fighting cats
in the heat once it was lit.
Every stick became
fire's friend—we'd watch for blue caves in the depths of them
learnt to turn the logs just so
hot side out.
Every morning the frost
fitted onto everything—leaves,
cars and slithered onto roads.
The dog's breath came out like dragons
our own caught light
and made rainbows.
Each day we'd mitten and sheepskin
knitted into buttons of coats and necessary scarves
but still those cold cold feet at school
and fingers that didn't bother us 'til
they turned blue at the tips
and made us scream.
Rain and more rain, the creek's flooded pleasure and booted we'd send
a load of fledgling boats to meet their doom to the white water.
Then hot water bottle dreaming
in flannel sheets.
It was like this all the time.

Blood

This morning's wash is full of
the iron tang scent
all the fabric whiteners
can't soften it from the clothes.

I hope the sunlight will set it right
but if they say you stink at school
tell them it was your mother
bleeding through the night,

tell them you are all made from it.

For The World To Swing

For the world to swing
you need to keep still
hoard those moments
lined up in one place and
let the tree rise up behind you
let the leaves go on growing
let your feet fall just there
so that sunlight makes shadows of them
and your hair falls down and
tickles your cheek.

There is only so much time
so much time.

Wildflower Seed Mix

Each child held a smudge of possibility on their hands;
seeds so tiny, how could they become whole plants?
Daisies whose flowers could dry out and crackle in their palms
the swishing wish of wattle, red brushes or blue stars?
One after the other and sometimes together
the children flung them—seeds, husk, the dried earth of their digging—
into the loose patch of soil and waited a moment
to see if they would grow.

River Child

She lifts feet
so river won't swallow
all those shapes
her eyes make
in rippling
chlorophyll water.

Pollen rests on water skin
and so for a while does her mind;
smooth unfurling
river's possibilities
song of it
calls her from right below the breastbone.

She'll learn the moment
just before diving
to expect
that smack of cold
pressing in from every direction.

But now, here's the water
clasping over and
hiding all her toes,
greener than a forest's secret
running easily into the future.

Sea Child

The sky's serrated, a fine
lined anchor hold
above his head

he leans
into the wind his life
for a moment hooked on

something concentrated there
what is it? The water eats
the shadow it casts

all the commotion of sea
and black wavelets are swifter
than this small surfacing thing

what is it? Will it come ashore,
eat the possible futures,
tilt there enticing his

thoughts back to the water
like slick fur swimming
thicker than a fish

too languid for log.
It rolls in the water
reminds him

He is the unknown,
this place
is pulsing
his bloodstream.

Sky Child

My child, it was slow:
I watched

this eyelid in the morning
fold open

back to closed
for sun dip horizon

night's tremble
lidded
shadow. Then, I saw

how hands formed birds
that slipped into
the grace of new space

could seem to perch atop
or dive from safety of nests,

joining in the world's song
chirping *i'm here, look, here*

balanced, careless
held by wind's breath.

If you fall you will swoop
musical light, a feather in sky.

Rabbit on the Moon

You see it there
settled with its ears alert
grey among the luminous
sequins of light

—everything is made of atoms,
everything but photons.
You see that rabbit
lope across your mind

a refracted figure
your thought's own darling
nibbling the lunar stalks,
moonbeams stripped of their

leaves and roots, shortened
into haphazard angles
while all those holes and craters
certainly the warren work of this

twitching velvet friend.
'See his ears?' you say
'See the way he's sitting?
Can't you see him too?'

Washing in Winter

        And sometimes—I will tell you—I sat and
waited for the washing to dry
in the last slit of sunlight
before the cold came cramping down.

Listen: birds go mad with the day's final calls.

          The neighbourhood magnified:
     a child's song; a door slams and the song stops sudden.
           Dogs take the opportunity
         to stretch their voices out to moonrise

before frost flowers all over everything
leaving thrills of ice like algal bloom
on the sheets, on hedges, fences
shoes left on our windowsill.

            My song goes:
       May the birds call out your name,
      may your clothes go ice-dry clean
       and all your dogs come home.

Iron My Breath

For you, I iron my breath,
dust the flames from my shoes
grapple with my own fingers and their workings.
I go and finish sewing the apples back to the tree
blossoms to my lip
sprinkle flour on the floor of our kitchen
and dance,
dance until we all return.
For you I will tie down my tongue
loosen my eyes
avert my palms.
It will be my job to fade the tiredness in the sunlight,
my duty to bulb each lantern
polish polish polish all the tiniest tears:
you must do your own breathing
to wear all my trying down.

Before You Sleep

Let your ears listen out;
crickets strumming their bodies,
a passing car
dog, voices low in the coming dark.
Between each breath a circle of quiet.
Let that stay there as you breathe in
in that round second
linger there and think of colours
in sunlit water
but don't forget to breathe out.
Think of fish, of the way they water-breathe
how they fly in their otherworld under the sea.
You can dive in now.
Let your mind swim down,
bring it in close to you and let your skin
hold it, like this bed holds you
or even the sea those fish we saw.
Feel the covering, your feet, hands,
each cheek and let your tongue lie still.
Can you hear the surf of sleep?
Can you smell the dreams you are going to have
or feel them warm along your body?
Dreams will find you here.
The tide rises rises, falls away with you.

Coax

We nestle
and match—one the other's striking board
the sulphur flare of
our pitch

and burn.

I coax you to be heat,
feed you pine needles and
you are fierce in your concentration
you consume these questions, these answers
these encoded woody stems
that once held blossoms.

As you turn and the light is
creeping from you so your face
is a beacon and as blinding
there; you are me with that glittering eye.
I have known you like myself
you have thrown flame
all along my secrets.

PART 3
FLIGHT FROM GRAVITY

Apostle Bird

She the red-eyed girl-bird
will appear her nest with
mud from these wheel ruts;

clean her beak against
other smears to an exact
o for her egg-home.

Up her flight pitches -
to a horizontal branch,
selected for its fine lack of angle:

she and her half-sisters smooth
ooze with their tongues
cementing in sunlight and leaf-shade.

Then they sit day, night, day
calling out names for morning,
with whistles angling, branching

new scales, new down, new apostles
to fill the world up with descending songs,
leaf-litter scratching

and woken eyes;
finding ways to lick the mud while
spreading the word of their wings.

Crow

I hail the wind. Before I transformed from a daughter—we were always of the egg. Bluer than the lake, a few shades lighter. I hail the wind, but I will not follow its instruction. With my feathers I winnow the direction, I sift it for my intentions. It cannot take me, the way I take flight from gravity. Burned I was. Burned more than Magpie who kept her voice. Burned I was. Burned more than Currawong who calls evening into being and plots all night with the fire still in her eye. The sky stuck in my eye. In my haste to flee that fire I took skywards and the spell fell through the crackling air. It took my girl-dom. It took my long possum hair. Now I am feathered. Now I am as coal, with my feathers glistening blue from the sky's last kiss as I transformed. I call to my mother, forgive my jealous heart. I call to my father, make me whole again. But to you, to you I say: feed me your children. For with this transformation, gone is my shame. I will eat their hearts and sing my short votive song to their deaths. I have always hailed the wind, the one that took the fire up and threw me into its midst. It has scattered me, shattered me, made me what I am.

Magpie

Hunter of the underground
with your voice regurgitating sunlight,

yet you carry those shadows on your back
—these noirs and flashes—
which almost seem to
scribe quick notes
flute clean
crisp morning tumble
and that warning call
ringing concentric, skirting your tree.

Worshippers carve your
totem into their footprints
hushing children *Listen*
listen to the song
ripping the light and dark to shreds.

Listen
for the September cracking
of the mottle blue eggs.

Telling them: *Avoid nearing nestlings*
or risk the switch to war-bird beak-bomb
fierce in protection of smokey fledges
buried in stick-weave home.

All this for bare-tremulous notes,
when grey infant feathers fail (after asking and asking)
there is the clarity.
True song burble creek flow narrow passing.
Bird law.

Rooster

Perhaps the rooster crows—
not to welcome the sun
or pull the day out the its bath of darkness—
but in gratitude
for the slippery world
shining clear
as a bird's short life.

Cat

You beat the night off your claws
fit fur one hair to another
like a woven thing—but sinew.
Your trembling purr is a decoy;
the eye in the face, a warning.
Win all the fights with your fang monster impression.
Take all the queens with your arching quick tail fling.
You banish tremor, kill with decisions.
One tick to the next, minutes are kittens
that need you and need you until you leave them;
slink dark thing of the dark along the walks
you know and knew and that know you
the way you can fall
bashing up time with the softest foot falls.

Dog

Tongue over
philtrum licker
pink stretches long
soft comforter
wet making -
a whine carpet
a woof-thruster of
dog speak.

Dogs are all day
no need for that
old word trick—
of knowing noise
is not equal to doing and
can frighten away
essence like rain
pulls at raw scent.

A look or lick,
a thump of tail
might be more—
to those who are
moment-ready
alive to gesture, nuance,
ear prick and
nose winkle—
than tongued-up voice noise.

Borer

All in one day these tiny circles marking the toothsome tree
up until it was bitter or too hard to pulp or the bark grew tight
back then, to the soft filaments, fibers just tough enough
the tree's own pattern back and forth like scratching.
If you were lost in the tree's long calendar
of up and out and restless leaves being tinkered by the wind
maybe there was a song, there, too, sung slow supersonic
A wood mite's lullaby. Sleep will come and borrow you.
Look at the flower you carved as a larvae; look at the petal
the stalk the tree's own beginning and its reason.

Snake

Cool soft
      circles of muscle
           catch of tongue
           clasp of nose
   flicks and pulls
time clicks slower
    eyes drops twinkle

         water drops of scales
            circle his eye
                  flick the clicks of time
           reflects his clasp
       sinew of tongue
   the soft nose of
      cool catch slower

           sinew as water
              time is soft dropping
                 the catch of eye
                      the muscle flick
               circles slower
            reflection pulls
        like a dry cool
     tongue.

Amanita Muscaria

Preening gills
whiter than stars
blithe in the shade
so fruiting body
so labial
and yet
the musk scent
of upturned moss and
the slow slow thrust
of such a creature
pointing heavenward
as if made of old sunlight
as we all are.

The sun will take back
the delicate folding
so soon the poisonous grandeur
sinks back to soil
and another year
will know the offspring
rising from loamy gravesites
hovering up
to inherit the earth.

In Black

That summer we loved a small black dog
whose eyes always seemed to
see beyond the immediate—
moving her neck from our stroking
to examine the future-hazed distance.

She lay by the door, always found the shaded places,
the tunnel through the honeysuckle, the trough
under the verandah where coolness pooled
musty, in the old dairy dark.

She would come when we called,
out into the light, her eyes half-closed
her muzzle dusted
and she would let us stroke
—with our sticky children's hands—
her earth-cooled fur.

Yam Dream

Desert tongues
short fingers
together the flames
children's soft kissable heads
or sperm in the dark with tiny lightbulbs
seeds and seeds and masses of them flawless
fault lines undulation
skin
ourselves unzipped to spirit level
taken in the night
moved from ghost to ghost
at cellular zoom.

Spurge

Spring and uncoil asparagus green
out-run spangled buds
tip atop spiral
pelting out pollens soporific
undone green gills
flutter in compound eyes of
monsters that buzz into frills
spurts of stalking
factual photosynthesis
phloem proliferate,
poking into sprung.

Jet Plane Year

The jet plane year
left streaks across the sky
(above hefty cumulus
all shadow-wrinkles)
this smear of time
unfastens its hold
(even on itself)
and returns to water drops
that take less than a second
to hit the ground.

PART 4
LUMINOUS THINGS

Four

After 'Four In The Morning' by Wislawa Szymorska

The hour of is it soon?
The hour of is it later?
The hour of the child's call, the old cat shifts position, the blanket tumbles
   to the floor.

The hour of where is the moon?
The hour of dispensing with the rational dream.
The hour of early joggers.

It is the hour when the mouse gives birth under the loose floorboard
wind makes branches operatic in the quiet.

An hour of mistrust that the sun will break night,
daylight will return.

The hour of anxious clench that no-one sees or hears;
the lives of others take form across the threshold of ourselves

until I swear, I dreamt your dream.
Let night end, let it all be over, let day - whatever it will bring - take place.

Dusk (Sundowner's Syndrome)
After 'Dusk in Winter' by W.S.Merwin

If the sun is friendless now, so am I.
How can he leave this way with no promises, no assurances, no goodbyes
just a blaze of fire on the canvassy sky?
I tremble for his return
try to accustom to the muzzle of dark that purrs, growls or both
the long way to morning.

Zero

*After 'A Narrow Fellow in the Grass'
by Emily Dickinson*

When I was a boy—and yet and yet
a close bright eye
the overlap of slink

I did not stop my leap or get
the full length of him burnt on my eye
or think

just leapt all muscle just like his
and to leap a full leap ---
the sky laughed down then set

me homewards with no plan where to fly
when I was a boy
and he sun-basked

stayed where he was to get
the full charge pulse
of a warm spring day.

Breaking

After 'Daybreak' by Galway Kinnell

Are those stars walking on a million tiny feet across the pebbled beachey sky? Do they dare into the sea with its tidal pull rhythm? Their line of time is that small ridge of sand on the flats where one after another the waves unroll their spindrift prayer mats. Watch them, these old ones, cross the wrinkled line from day to night, water to dry, surfing where their sticky toes no longer touch the wavered floor —see them hold out their five arms and swim-wash as each rug pulls from underneath—out into open water. There, they might meet again, strung along new horizons breaking open the sky's perforations.

Divers

After 'Loons Mating' by David Wagoner

Qualified both for water and air
the two of them lose the eye to become surface
in oily water light
rippled at the throat and rippled in their call
wings break to flight.

They make spaces between them
turn uprisen as
wing ready wind
carriage and wheel
with knowledge their bodies compound.

They do not sing of the nest, eggs, long wait for hatching,
this comes as dawn breaks open
sky calls them beautiful
quivery undulation at shore and further out
haunting haunted calling for applause.

Pears

After 'Study of Two Pears' by Wallace Stevens

1.

Shadows stretch as bell-curve
underside their solidity
darker pools.

2.

One dimpled buttock each
no legs but stems broken where
they kissed/were kissed by trees.

3.

They fume with sweetness
dot to dot tattoo yellow skins
belly flesh their pendulums.

4.

What they are not: flat, opalescent, papery
warm or protruding
heavy, glistening or hard.

5.

They belong outdoors with birds
beaking their softness
into furrows.

6.

They belong juicily consumed.
They belong tree dongles
boinging onto grassland.

7.
Found fragrant and gnawable
gold promises of sleep
inverted wet on the fur-lip.

8.
Sliced, they belong to fingers of orchard
once flower now eaten by
rough love; but seeded.

Muso Soseki

After 'Magnificent Peak' by Muso Soseki

Mountains rise as if on the intake
    upwards they go
        summiting on filling swells
           of rock.
                We of lung/ muscle/ bone
                              need clean air to rise ourselves,

    breathe quicker and die sooner.

        Seventy million years later,
                the Earth exhales.

Afterword

Sometimes a poem echoes with strange premonition. Take 'Crow' for instance. There I was in a workshop, notebook balanced on my knee, trying to write something 'figurative' about something ordinary. It was 2018. It had rained recently. Almost a year later, in the summer of 2019/20 when it seemed that it would never rain again I sent that poem to Cordite, and it was released in February just when bushfires were in the forefront of everyone in Australia's consciousness—that burning crisp voice that spoke that poem rattled me when I re-read it. It seemed to know all about the fires. It spoke of the pain and transformation of being burnt. Was that really mine? How did that poem know what was about to happen?

Here I am now, writing an afterword to about 10 years of writing poems—sometimes every day, which is when they get really rich—but mostly sporadically fitting them into daily life. It's lockdown here, the streets are eerily quiet of cars, but people are out exercising and walking the dog. That crow poem says 'feed me your children' but perhaps it could just as well have been, feed me your parents. Feed me the vulnerable. Feed me the poor and the lonely.

The poems are preoccupied with splitting the ordinary open to reveal what's extraordinary under the surface. I say 'the poems' because they seem to take me there, wherever there is. Under the ordinary experience of having your own children in the world is the absolute gobsmackery that they exist at all. Under the ordinary workings of the natural world is the shocking realisation that there is not always language to describe its intricate workings.

Under the ordinary plying of words into sequence is the remarkable position they leave one another in.

Acknowledgements

With special thanks to Jen Crawford, Melinda Smith and Jen Webb as well as the Poetry Stream group from Between the Lines 2019. Thanks also go to the poets of the Prose Poetry Collective and 365+1, as well as all those who have followed the blog *Poemation*. Thanks to the Hardcoven 2019 and the Hardcopy alumni—particularly Nigel Featherstone and the team from the ACT Writer's Centre. Thanks go out to the organisers and participants of That Poetry Thing at Smith's Alternative. Lastly, thanks are due to Gorman + Ainslie Arts centre staff and residents who have supported me with space and time to work.

'Wildflower Seed Mix'—runner up in the Action Bus Poetry Award, 2013.

'Naked Song'—appeared in *Meniscus*, 2017.

'Prose Poems'—early drafts written as part of the Prose Poetry Collective, 2018 and 2019.

'Childpoems' (part 4) were selected from my poetry blog, *Poemation*, where earlier drafts of these poems appeared. (https://poemation.wordpress.com)

'If Prose is a House' and 'The Mother Poems'—early drafts of these poems appeared as part of 365+1 poem a day challenge for 3 months in 2017.

'Crow'—appeared in *Cordite 'Earth',* 2020.

'Perhaps the Rooster'/ 'Dog'/ 'Cat'/ 'In Black'/ 'Yam Dream'/ 'Dead All This Time'/ 'Jet Plane Year'—early drafts appeared on *Poemation*.

'Apostle Bird'/ 'Sacred Magpie'/ 'Spurge'/ 'Woodflower' / 'Snake'/ 'Amanita'—early drafts appeared in *365+1*.

'Swift'—appeared in *Meniscus*, 2019.

'Strokes of Light'—appears in *Meniscus*, 2019, and *In Your Hands*, Red Room Poetry, 2020.

'Skull' and 'Pinch'—*TEXT,* 2020 (forthcoming).

About the author

Lucy is a writer and poet. She works from a studio at Gorman + Ainslie Arts Centre. In 2019 she was a HardCopy non-fiction stream participant for her quirky manuscript *Calling Your Dog*. She also received an ArtsACT grant to be mentored by Isobelle Carmody for her work of fiction *Mela's Aqueduct* in collaboration with digital artist Paul Summerfield. Her poems have recently appeared in *Cordite* and *Meniscus,* and reviews in *Verity La*. She lives in a happy menagerie with her four kids and loving husband.

www.ingramcontent.com/pod-product-compliance
Lightning Source LLC
Chambersburg PA
CBHW032050290426
44110CB00012B/1034